# Martyred Armenia

Fà'iz El-Ghusein

**Martyred Armenia**

Copyright © 2014 Indo-European Publishing

Contact:
IndoEuropeanPublishing@gmail.com

The present edition is a reproduction of 1918 publication of this work. Minor typographical errors may have been corrected without note, however, for an authentic reading experience the spelling, punctuation, and capitalization have been retained from the original text.

ISBN: 978-1-60444-789-7

# FOREWORD

I am a Bedouin, a son of one of the Heads of the tribe of El-Sulût, who dwell in El-Lejât, in the Haurân territory. Like other sons of tribal Chiefs, I entered the Tribal School at Constantinople, and subsequently the Royal College. On the completion of my education, I was attached to the staff of the Vali of Syria (or Damascus), on which I remained for a long while. I was then Kaimakâm of Mamouret-el-Azîz (Kharpout), holding this post for three and a half years, after which I practised as a lawyer at Damascus, my partners being Shukri Bey El-Asli and Abdul-Wahhâb Bey El-Inglîzi. I next became a member of the General Assembly at that place, representing Haurân, and later a member of the Committee of that Assembly. On the outbreak of the war, I was ordered to resume my previous career, that is, the duties of Kaimakâm, but I did not comply, as I found the practice of the law more advantageous in many ways and more tranquil.

I was denounced by an informer as being a delegate of a Society constituted in the Lebanon with the object of achieving the independence of the Arab people, under the protection of England and France, and of inciting the tribes against the Turkish Government. On receipt of this denunciation, I was arrested by the Government, thrown into prison, and subsequently sent in chains, with a company of police and gendarmes, to Aalîya, where persons accused of political offences were tried. I was acquitted, but as the Government disregarded the decisions given in such cases, and was resolved on the removal and destruction of all enlightened Arabs—

1

whatever the circumstances might be—it was thought necessary that I should be despatched to Erzeroum, and Jemâl Pasha sent me thither with an officer and five of the regular troops. When I reached Diarbekir, Hasan Kaleh, at Erzeroum, was being pressed by the Russians, and the Vali of Diarbekir was ordered to detain me at that place.

After twenty-two days' confinement in prison for no reason, I was released; I hired a house and remained at Diarbekir for six and a half months, seeing and hearing from the most reliable sources all that took place in regard to the Armenians, the majority of my informants being superior officers and officials, or Notables of Diarbekir and its dependencies, as well as others from Van, Bitlis, Mamouret-el-Azîz, Aleppo and Erzeroum. The people of Van had been in Diarbekir since the occupation of their territory by the Russians, whilst the people and officials of Bitlis had recently emigrated thither. Many of the Erzeroum officers came to Diarbekir on military or private business, whilst Mamouret-el-Azîz was near by, and many people came to us from thence. As I had formerly been a Kaimakâm in that Vilayet, I had a large acquaintance there and heard all the news. More especially, the time which I passed in prison with the heads of the tribes in Diarbekir enabled me to study the movement in its smallest details. The war must needs come to an end after a while, and it will then be plain to readers of this book that all I have written is the truth, and that it contains only a small part of the atrocities committed by the Turks against the hapless Armenian people.

After passing this time at Diarbekir I fled, both to escape from captivity and from fear induced by what had befallen me from some of the fanatical Turks. After great sufferings, during which I was often exposed to death and

2

slaughter, I reached Basra, and conceived the idea of publishing this book, as a service to the cause of truth and of a people oppressed by the Turks, and also, as I have stated at the close, to defend the faith of Islam against the charge of fanaticism which will be brought against it by Europeans. May God guide us in the right way.

I have written this preface at Bombay, on the 1st of September, 1916.

FÀ'IZ EL-GHUSEIN

# MARTYRED ARMENIA

# THE NARRATIVE

Outline of Armenian History.—In past ages the Armenian race was, like other nations, not possessed of an autonomous government, until God bestowed upon them a man, named Haig, a bold leader, who united the Armenians and formed them into an independent state. This took place before the Christian era. The nation preserved their independence for a considerable time, reaching the highest point of their glory and prosperity under their king Dikrân, who constituted the city of Dikrânokerta—Diarbekir—the capital of his Government. Armenia remained independent in the time of the Romans, extending her rule over a part of Asia Minor and Syria, and a portion of Persia, but, in consequence of the protection afforded by the Armenians to certain kings who were hostile to Rome, the Romans declared war against her, their troops entered her capital, and from that time Armenian independence was lost. The country remained tossing on the waves of despotism, now independent, now subjected to foreign rule, until its conquest by the Arabs and subsequently by the Ottoman power.

The Armenian Population.—The number of the Armenians in Ottoman territory does not exceed 1,900,000 souls. I have borrowed this figure from a book by a Turkish writer, who states that it is the official computation made by the Government previous to the Balkan war; he estimates the Armenians residing in Roumelia at 400,000, those in Ottoman Asia at 1,500,000. The Armenians in Russia and Persia are said not to exceed 3,000,000, thus bringing the

4

total number of Armenians in the world to over four and a half millions.

The Vilayets Inhabited by Armenians.—The Vilayets inhabited by Armenians are Diarbekir, Van, Bitlis, Erzeroum, Mamouret-el-Azîz, Sivas, Adana, Aleppo, Trebizond, Broussa, and Constantinople. The numbers in Van, Bitlis, Adana, Diarbekir, Erzeroum, and Kharpout were greater than those in the other Vilayets, but in all cases they were fewer than the Turks and Kurds, with the exception of Van and Bitlis, where they were equal or superior in number. In the province of Moush (Vilayet of Bitlis) they were more numerous than the Kurds; all industry and commerce in those parts was in Armenian hands; their agriculture was more prosperous; they were much more advanced than the Turks and Kurds in those Vilayets; and the large number of their schools, contrasted with the few schools of their alien fellow countrymen, is a proof of their progress and of the decline of the other races.

Armenian Societies.—The Armenians possess learned and political Societies, the most important of which are the "Tashnagtziân" and the "Hunchak." The programme of these two Societies is to make every effort and adopt every means to attain that end from which no Armenian ever swerves, namely, administrative independence under the supervision of the Great Powers of Europe. I have enquired of many Armenians whom I have met, but I have not found one who said that he desired political independence, the reason being that in most of the Vilayets which they inhabit the Armenians are less numerous than the Kurds, and if they became independent the advantage to the Kurds would be greater than to themselves. Hitherto, the Kurds have been in a very degraded state of ignorance;

5

disorder is supreme in their territory, and the cities are in ruins. The Armenians, therefore, prefer to remain under Turkish rule, on condition that the administration is carried on under the supervision of the Great European Powers, as they place no confidence in the promises of the Turks, who take back to-day what they bestowed yesterday. These two Societies thus earnestly labour for the propagation of this view amongst the Armenians, and for the attainment of their object by every means. I have been told by an Armenian officer that one of these Societies proposes to attain its end by means of internal revolts, but the policy of the second is to do so by peaceful means only.

The above is a brief summary of the policy of these Societies. It is said, however, that the programme of one of them aims at Armenian political independence.

Any who desire further details as to Armenian history or societies should refer to their historical books.

The Armenian Massacres.—History does not record that the Kurds, fellow-countrymen of the Armenians in the Vilayets inhabited by both peoples, rose in conflict with the latter, or that the Kurds plundered the property of the Armenians, or outraged their women, until the year 1888, when they rose by order of the Turkish Government and slaughtered Armenians in Van, Kharpout, Erzeroum, and Moush. Again, in the time of Abdul-Hamîd II., in 1896, when the Armenians rose and entered the Ottoman Bank at Constantinople, with the object of frightening the Sultan and compelling him to proclaim the Constitution, he ordered a massacre at Constantinople and in the Vilayets. But hitherto there has been no instance of the people of Turkey proceeding to the slaughter of Armenians

6

on a general scale unless incited and constrained to do so by the Government. In the massacre of 1896, 15,000 were killed in Constantinople itself, and 300,000 in the Vilayets.

Armenians were also killed in the Vilayet of Adana, some months after the proclamation of the Constitution, but this slaughter did not extend beyond the two Vilayets of Adana and Aleppo, where the influence of Abdul-Hamîd was paramount till the year 1909. I do not, however, find any detailed account of this massacre, or any information as to the numbers killed.

The goods and cattle of the Armenians were plundered, and their houses wrecked, more especially in the slaughter of 1896, but many of their countrymen[1] protected them and concealed them in their houses from the officials of the Government.

The Government consistently inflamed the Moslem Kurds and Turks against them, making use of the Faith of Islam as a means to attain their object in view of the ignorance of the Mohammedans as to the true laws of their religion.

Declaration of the Ottoman Government.—"Inasmuch as the Armenians are committing acts opposed to the laws and taking advantage of all occasions to disturb the Government; as they have been found in possession of prohibited arms, bombs, and explosive materials, prepared with the object of internal revolt; as they have killed Moslems in Van, and have aided the Russian armies at a time when the Government is in a state of war with England, France, and Russia; and in the apprehension

---

[1] Presumably amongst the Turks and Kurds.—Translator.

7

that the Armenians may, as is their habit, lend themselves to seditious tumult and revolt; the Government have decreed that all the Armenians shall be collected and despatched to the Vilayets of Mosul, Syria, and Deir-el-Zûr, their persons, goods and honour being safeguarded. The necessary orders have been given for ensuring their comfort, and for their residence in those territories until the termination of the war."

Such is the official declaration of the Ottoman Government in regard to the Armenians. But the secret resolution was that companies of militia should be formed to assist the gendarmes in the slaughter of the Armenians, that these should be killed to the last man, and that the work of murder and destruction should take place under the supervision of trusty agents of the Unionists, who were known for their brutality. Reshîd Bey was appointed to the Vilayet of Diarbekir and invested with extensive powers, having at his disposal a gang of notorious murderers, such as Ahmed Bey El-Serzi, Rushdi Bey, Khalîl Bey, and others of this description.

The reason for this decision, as it was alleged, was that the Armenians residing in Europe and in Egypt had sent twenty of their devoted partisans to kill Talaat, Enver, and others of the Unionist leaders; the attempt had failed, as a certain Armenian, a traitor to his nation and a friend of Bedri Bey, the Chief of the Public Security at Constantinople (or according to others, Azmi Bey), divulged the matter and indicated the Armenian agents, who had arrived at Constantinople. The latter were arrested and executed, but secretly, in order that it might not be said that there were men attempting to kill the heads of the Unionist Society.

Another alleged reason also was that certain Armenians, whom the Government had collected from the Vilayets of Aleppo and Adrianople and had sent off to complete their military service, fled, with their arms, to Zeitoun, where they assembled, to the number of sixty young men, and commenced to resist the Government and to attack wayfarers. The Government despatched a military force under Fakhry Pasha, who proceeded to the spot, destroyed a part of Zeitoun, and killed men, women and children, without encountering opposition on the part of the Armenians. He collected the men and women and sent them off with parties of troops, who killed many of the men, whilst as for the women, do not ask what was their fate. They were delivered over to the Ottoman soldiery; the children died of hunger and thirst; not a man or woman reached Syria except the halt and blind, who were unable to keep themselves alive; the young men were all slaughtered; and the good-looking women fell into the hands of the Turkish youths.

Emigrants from Roumelia were conveyed to Zeitoun and established there, the name of that place being changed to "Reshadîya," so that nothing should remain to remind the Turks of the Armenian name. During our journey from Hamah we saw many Armenian men and women, sitting under small tents which they had constructed from sheets, rugs, etc. Their condition was most pitiable, and how could it be otherwise? Many of these had been used to sit only on easy chairs [lit., rocking-chairs], amid luxurious furniture, in houses built in the best style, well arranged and splendidly furnished. I saw, as others saw also, many Armenian men and women in goods-wagons on the railway between Aleppo and Hamah, herded together in a way which moved compassion.

After my arrival at Aleppo, and two days' stay there, we took the train to a place called Ser-Arab-Pounâri. I was accompanied by five Armenians, closely guarded, and despatched to Diarbekir. We walked on our feet thence to Serûj, where we stopped at a khân [rest-house] filled with Armenian women and children, with a few sick men. These women were in a deplorable state, as they had done the journey from Erzeroum on foot, taking a long while to arrive at Serûj. I talked with them in Turkish, and they told me that the gendarmes with them had brought them to places where there was no water, refusing to tell them where water was to be found until they had received money as the price. Some of them, who were pregnant, had given birth on the way, and had abandoned their infants in the uninhabited wastes. Most of these women had left their children behind, either in despair, or owing to illness or weakness which made them unable to carry them, so they threw them on the ground; some from natural affection could not do this and so perished in the desert, not parted from their infants. They told me that there were some among them who had not been used to walk for a single hour, having been brought up in luxury, with men to wait on them and women to attend them. These had fallen into the hands of the Kurds, who recognize no divine law, and who live on lofty mountains and in dense forests like beasts of prey; their honour was outraged and they died by brutal violence, many of them killing themselves rather than sacrifice their virtue to these ravening wolves.

We then proceeded in carts from Serûj to El-Raha (Urfa). On the way I saw crowds going on foot, whom from a distance I took for troops marching to the field of battle. On approaching, I found they were Armenian women, walking barefoot and weary, placed in ranks like the gendarmes who preceded and followed them. Whenever one of them lagged behind, a gendarme would beat her with the butt of his rifle, throwing her on her face, till she rose terrified and rejoined her companions. But if one lagged from sickness, she was either abandoned, alone in the wilderness, without help or comfort, to be a prey to wild beasts, or a gendarme ended her life by a bullet.

On arrival at Urfa, we learned that the Government had sent a force of gendarmes and police to the Armenian quarters of the town to collect their arms, subsequently dealing with these people as with others. As they were aware of what had happened to their kinsmen—the khâns at Urfa being full of women and children—they did not give up their arms, but showed armed resistance, killing one man of the police and three gendarmes. The authorities of Urfa applied for a force from Aleppo, and by order of Jemâl Pasha—the executioner of Syria—Fakhry Pasha came with cannon. He turned the Armenian quarters into a waste place, killing the men and the children, and great numbers of the women, except such as yielded themselves to share the fate of their sisters—expulsion on foot to Deir-el-Zûr, after the Pasha and his officers had selected the prettiest amongst them. Disease was raging among them; they were outraged by the Turks and Kurds; and hunger and thirst completed their extermination.

After leaving Urfa, we again saw throngs of women, exhausted by fatigue and misery, dying of hunger and thirst, and we saw the bodies of the dead lying by the roadside.

On our arrival at a place near a village called Kara Jevren, about six hours distant from Urfa, we stopped at a spring

11

to breakfast and drink. I went a little apart, towards the source, and came upon a most appalling spectacle. A woman, partly unclothed, was lying prone, her chemise disordered and red with blood, with four bullet-wounds in her breast. I could not restrain myself, but wept bitterly. As I drew out a handkerchief to wipe away my tears, and looked round to see whether any of my companions had observed me, I saw a child not more than eight years old, lying on his face, his head cloven by an axe. This made my grief the more vehement, but my companions cut short my lamentations, for I heard the officer, Aarif Effendi, calling to the priest Isaac, and saying, "Come here at once," and I knew that he had seen something which had startled him. I went towards him, and what did I behold? Three children lying in the water, in terror of their lives from the Kurds, who had stripped them of their clothes and tortured them in various ways, their mother near by, moaning with pain and hunger. She told us her story, saying that she was from Erzeroum, and had been brought by the troops to this place with many other women after a journey of many days. After they had been plundered of money and clothing, and the prettiest women had been picked out and handed over to the Kurds, they reached this place, where Kurdish men and women collected and robbed them of all the clothes that remained on them. She herself had stayed here, as she was sick and her children would not leave her. The Kurds came upon them again and left them naked. The children had lain in the water in their terror, and she was at the point of death. The priest collected some articles of clothing and gave them to the woman and the children; the officer sent a man to the post of gendarmes which was near by, and ordered the gendarme whom the man brought with him to send on the woman and children to Urfa, and to bury the bodies which were near the guardhouse. The sick woman told me that the dead woman refused to yield herself to outrage, so they killed her and she died nobly, chaste and pure from defilement; to induce her to yield they killed her son beside her, but she was firm in her resolve and died heart-broken.

In the afternoon we went on towards Kara Jevren, and one of the drivers pointed out to us some high mounds, surrounded by stones and rocks, saying that here Zohrâb and Vartakis had been killed, they having been leading Notables among the Armenians, and their Deputies.

Krikôr Zohrâb and Vartakis.—No one is ignorant of who and what was Zohrâb, the Armenian Deputy for Constantinople, his name and repute being celebrated after the institution of the Chamber. He used to speak with learning and reflection, refuting objections by powerful arguments and convincing proofs. His speeches in the Chamber were mostly conclusive. He was learned in all subjects, but especially in the science of law, as he was a graduate of universities and had practised at the Bar for many years. He was endowed with eloquence and great powers of exposition; he was courageous, not to be turned from his purpose or intimidated from pursuing his national aims. When the Unionists realised that they were deficient in knowledge, understanding nothing about polity or administration, and not aware of the meaning of liberty or constitutional government, they resolved to return to the system of their Tartar forefathers, the devastation of cities and the slaughter of innocent men, as it was in that direction that their powers lay. They sent Zohrâb and his colleague Vartakis away from Constantinople, with orders that they should be killed on the way, and it was announced that they had been murdered by a band of brigands. They killed them in order that it might not be said that Armenians were more powerful, more learned, and more intelligent than Turks. Why should such bands murder none but Armenians? The falsity of the statement is obvious.

Zohrâb and Vartakis fell victims to their own courage and firmness of purpose; they were killed out of envy of their learning and their love for their own people, and for their tenacity in pursuing their own path. They were killed by that villain, Ahmed El-Serzi, one of the sworn men of the Unionists, he who murdered Zeki Bey; his story in the Ottoman upheaval is well known, and how the Unionists saved him from his fitting punishment and even from prison. A Kurd told me that Vartakis was one of the boldest and most courageous men who ever lived; he was chief of the Armenian bands in the time of Abdul-Hamîd; he was wounded in the foot by a cannon-ball whilst the Turkish troops were pursuing these bands, and was imprisoned either at Erzeroum or at Maaden, in the Vilayet of Diarbekir. The Sultan Abdul-Hamîd, through his officials, charged him to modify his attitude and acknowledge that he had been in error, when he should be pardoned and appointed to any post he might choose. He rejected this offer, saying, "I will not sell my conscience for a post, or say that the Government of Abdul-Hamîd is just, whilst I see its tyranny with my eyes and touch it with my hand."

It is said that the Unionists ordered that all the Armenian Deputies should be put to death, and the greater number of them were thus dealt with. It is reported also that Dikrân Gilikiân, the well-known writer, who was an adherent of the Committee of Union and Progress, was killed in return for his learning, capacity, and devotion to their cause. Such was the recompense of his services to the Unionists.

In the evening we arrived at Kara Jevren, and slept there till morning. At sunrise we went on towards Sivrek, and half-way on the road we saw a terrible spectacle. The corpses of the killed were lying in great numbers on both sides of the road; here we saw a woman outstretched on the ground, her body half veiled by her long hair; there, women lying on their faces, the dried blood blackening their delicate forms; there again, the corpses of men, parched to the semblance of charcoal by the heat of the sun. As we approached Sivrek, the corpses became more numerous, the bodies of children being in a great majority. As we arrived at Sivrek and left our carts, we saw one of the servants of the khân carrying a little infant with hair as yellow as gold, whom he threw behind the house. We asked him about it, and he said that there were three sick Armenian women in the house, who had lagged behind their companions, that one of them had given birth to this infant, but could not nourish it, owing to her illness. So it had died and been thrown out, as one might throw out a mouse.

Demand for Ransom.—Whilst we were at Sivrek, Aarif Effendi told me—after he had been at the Government offices—that the Commandant of Gendarmerie and the Chief of Police of that place had requested him to hand over to them the five Armenians who were with him, and that on his refusal they had insisted, saying that, if they were to reach Diarbekir in safety, they must pay a ransom of fifty liras for themselves. We went to the khân, where the officer summoned the priest Isaac and told him how matters stood. After speaking to his companions, the priest replied that they could pay only ten liras altogether,

15

as they had no more in their possession. When convinced by his words, the officer took the ten liras and undertook to satisfy the others.

This officer had a dispute with the Commandant of Gendarmerie at Aleppo, the latter desiring to take these five men on the grounds that they had been sent with a gendarme for delivery to his office. Ahmed Bey, the Chief of the Irregular band at Urfa, also desired to take them, but the officer refused to give them up to him—he being a member of the Committee of Union and Progress—and brought them in safety to Diarbekir.

After passing the night at Sivrek we left early in the morning. As we approached Diarbekir the corpses became more numerous, and on our route we met companies of women going to Sivrek under guard of gendarmes, weary and wretched, the traces of tears and misery plain on their faces—a plight to bring tears of blood from stones, and move the compassion of beasts of prey.

What, in God's name, had these women done? Had they made war on the Turks, or killed even one of them? What was the crime of these hapless creatures, whose sole offence was that they were Armenians, skilled in the management of their homes and the training of their children, with no thought beyond the comfort of their husbands and sons, and the fulfilment of their duties towards them.

I ask you, O Moslems—is this to be counted as a crime? Think for a moment. What was the fault of these poor women? Was it in their being superior to the Turkish women in every respect? Even assuming that their men had merited such treatment, is it right that these women

16

should be dealt with in a manner from which wild beasts would recoil? God has said in the Koran: "Do not load one with another's burthens," that is, Let not one be punished for another.

What had these weak women done, and what had their infants done? Can the men of the Turkish Government bring forward even a feeble proof to justify their action and to convince the people of Islam, who hold that action for unlawful and reject it? No; they can find no word to say before a people whose usages are founded on justice, and their laws on wisdom and reason.

Is it right that these imposters, who pretend to be the supports of Islam and the Khilâfat, the protectors of the Moslems, should transgress the command of God, transgress the Koran, the Traditions of the Prophet, and humanity? Truly, they have committed an act at which Islam is revolted, as well as all Moslems and all the peoples of the earth, be they Moslems, Christians, Jews, or idolators. As God lives, it is a shameful deed, the like of which has not been done by any people counting themselves as civilised.

The Infant in the Waste.—After we had gone a considerable distance we saw a child of not more than four years old, with a fair complexion, blue eyes, and golden hair, with all the indications of luxury and pampering, standing in the sun, motionless and speechless. The officer told the driver to stop the cart, got out alone, and questioned the child, who made no reply, and did not utter a word. The officer said: "If we take this child with us to Diarbekir, the authorities will take him from us, and he will share the fate of his people in being killed. It is best that we leave him. Perhaps God will move one of the Kurds to compassion, that he take him and bring him up." None of us could say anything to him; he entered the cart and we drove on, leaving the child as we found him, without speech, tears, or movement. Who knows of what rich man or Notable of the Armenians he was the son? He had hardly seen the light when he was orphaned by the slaughter of his parents and kinsmen. Those who should have carried him were weary of him— for the women were unable to carry even themselves—so they had abandoned him in the waste, far from human habitation. Man, who shows kindness to beasts, and forms societies for their protection, can be merciless to his own kind, more especially to infants who can utter no complaint; he leaves them under the heat of the sun, thirsty and famishing, to be devoured by wild creatures.

Leaving the boy, our hearts burning within us, and full of grief and anguish, we arrived before sunset at a khân some hours distant from Diarbekir. There we passed the night, and in the morning we went on amid the mangled forms of the slain. The same sight met our view on every side; a man lying, his breast pierced by a bullet; a woman torn open by lead; a child sleeping his last sleep beside his mother; a girl in the flower of her age, in a posture which told its own story. Such was our journey until we arrived at a canal, called Kara Pounâr, near Diarbekir, and here we found a change in the method of murder and savagery.

We saw here bodies burned to ashes. God, from whom no secrets are hid, knows how many young men and fair girls, who should have led happy lives together, had been consumed by fire in this ill-omened place.

We had expected not to find corpses of the killed near to the walls of Diarbekir, but we were mistaken, for we

18

journeyed among the bodies until we entered the city gate. As I was informed by some Europeans who returned from Armenia after the massacres, the Government ordered the burial of all the bodies from the roadside when the matter had become the subject of comment in European newspapers.

In Prison.—On our arrival at Diarbekir the officer handed us over to the authorities and we were thrown into prison, where I remained for twenty-two days. During this time I obtained full information about the movement from one of the prisoners, who was a Moslem of Diarbekir, and who related to me what had happened to the Armenians there. I asked him what was the reason of the affair, why the Government had treated them in this way, and whether they had committed any act calling for their complete extermination. He said that, after the declaration of war, the Armenians, especially the younger men, had failed to comply with the orders of the Government, that most of them had evaded military service by flight, and had formed companies which they called "Roof Companies." These took money from the wealthy Armenians for the purchase of arms, which they did not deliver to the authorities, but sent to their companies, until the leading Armenians and Notables assembled, went to the Government offices, and requested that these men should be punished as they were displeased at their proceedings.

I asked whether the Armenians had killed any Government official, or any Turks or Kurds in Diarbekir. He replied that they had killed no one, but that a few days after the arrival of the Vali, Reshîd Bey, and the Commandant of Gendarmerie, Rushdi Bey, prohibited arms had been found in some Armenian houses, and also in the church. On the discovery of these arms, the

Government summoned some of the principal Armenians and flung them into prison; the spiritual authorities made repeated representations, asking for the release of these men, but the Government, far from complying with the request, imprisoned the ecclesiastics also, the number of Notables thus imprisoned amounting to nearly seven hundred. One day the Commandant of Gendarmerie came and informed them that an Imperial Order had been issued for their banishment to Mosul, where they were to remain until the end of the war. They were rejoiced at this, procured all they required in the way of money, clothes, and furniture, and embarked on the keleks (wooden rafts resting on inflated skins, used by the inhabitants of that region for travelling on the Euphrates and Tigris) to proceed to Mosul. After a while it was understood that they had all been drowned in the Tigris, and that none of them had reached Mosul. The authorities continued to send off and kill the Armenians, family by family, men, women and children, the first families sent from Diarbekir being those of Kazaziân, Tirpanjiân, Minassiân, and Kechijiân, who were the wealthiest families in the place. Among the 700 individuals was a bishop named—as far as I recollect—Homandriâs; he was the Armenian Catholic Bishop, a venerable and learned old man of about eighty; they showed no respect to his white beard, but drowned him in the Tigris.

Megerditch, the Bishop-delegate of Diarbekir, was also among the 700 imprisoned. When he saw what was happening to his people he could not endure the disgrace and shame of prison, so he poured petroleum over himself and set it on fire. A Moslem, who was imprisoned for having written a letter to this bishop three years before the events, told me that he was a man of great courage and learning, devoted to his people, with no fear of death, but unable to submit to oppression and humiliation.

Some of the imprisoned Kurds attacked the Armenians in the gaol itself, and killed two or three of them out of greed for their money and clothing, but nothing was done to bring them to account. The Government left only a very small number of Armenians in Diarbekir, these being such as were skilled in making boots and similar articles for the army. Nineteen individuals had remained in the prison, where I saw and talked with them; these, according to the pretence of the authorities, were Armenian bravoes.

The last family deported from Diarbekir was that of Dunjiân, about November, 1915. This family was protected by certain Notables of the place, from desire for their money, or the beauty of some of their women.

Dikrân.—This man was a member of the central committee of the Tashnagtziân Society in Diarbekir. An official of that place, who belonged to the Society of Union and Progress, told me that the authorities seized Dikrân and demanded from him the names of his associates. He refused, and said that he could not give the names until the committee had met and decided whether or not it was proper to furnish this information to the Government. He was subjected to varieties of torture, such as putting his feet in irons till they swelled and he could not walk, plucking out his nails and eyelashes with a cruel instrument, etc., but he would not say a word, nor give the name of one of his associates. He was deported with the others and died nobly out of love for his nation, preferring death to the betrayal of the secrets of his brave people to the Government.

21

Aghôb Kaitanjiân.—Aghôb Kaitanjiân was one of the Armenians imprisoned on the charge of being bravoes of the Armenian Society in Diarbekir, and in whose possession explosive material had been found. I often talked to him, and I asked him to tell me his story. He said that one day, whilst he was sitting in his house, a police agent knocked at the door and told him that the Chief of Police wished to see him at his office. He went there, and some of the police asked him about the Armenian Society and its bravoes. He replied that he knew nothing of either societies or bravoes. He was then bastinadoed and tortured in various ways for several days till he despaired of life, preferring death to a continuance of degradation. He had a knife with him, and when they aggravated the torture so that he could endure it no longer, he asked them to let him go to the latrine and on his return he would tell them all he knew about the Armenian matter. With the help of the police he went, and cut the arteries of his wrists[2] ... with the object of committing suicide. The blood gushed out freely; he got to the door of the police-office and there fainted. They poured water on his face and he recovered consciousness; he was brought before the officer and the interrogatory was renewed.[3] ... The Chief of Police was confounded at this proceeding and sent him to the hospital until he was cured. I saw the wounds on his hands, and they were completely healed. This was the story as he told it to me himself. He desired me to publish it in an Armenian newspaper called Häyrenîk (Fatherland), which appears in America, in order that it may be read by his brother Garabet, now in that country, who had been convinced that the Government would leave none of them alive.

---

[2] Episodes in the original are here omitted.—Translator.
[3] Episodes in the original are here omitted.—Translator.

I associated freely with the young Armenians who were imprisoned, and we talked much of these acts, the like of which, as happening to a nation such as theirs, have never been heard of, nor recorded in the history of past ages. These youths were sent for trial by the court-martial at Kharpout, and I heard that they arrived there safely and asked permission to embrace the Moslem faith. This was to escape from contemptuous treatment by the Kurds, and not from the fear of death, as their conversion would not save them from the penalty if they were shown to deserve it. Before their departure they asked me what I had heard about them, and whether the authorities purposed to kill them on the way or not. After enquiring about this, and ascertaining that they would not be killed in this way, I informed them accordingly; they were rejoiced, saying that all they desired was to remain alive to see the results of the war. They said that the Armenians deserved the treatment which they had received, as they would never see the necessity for taking precautions against the Turks, believing that the constitutional Turkish Government would never proceed to measures of this kind without valid reason. The Government has perpetrated these deeds although no official, Kurd, Turk, or Moslem, has been killed by an Armenian, and we know not what the weighty reasons may have been which impelled them to so unprecedented a measure. And if the Armenians should not be reproached with a negligence for which they have paid dearly, yet a people who do not take full precautions are liable to be taxed justly with blameworthy carelessness.

My Travelling-Companions.—From time to time I visited the men who had been in my company during the journey, but after my release the director of the prison would not permit me to go to them. I used, therefore, to ask for one of them and talk with him outside the prison in which the Armenians were confined. After a while I enquired for them and was told that they had been sent to execution, like others before them, and at this I cried out in dismay. One day I saw a gendarme who had been imprisoned with us for a short time on the charge of having stolen articles from the effects of dead Armenians, and as he knew my companions I asked him about them. He said that he had killed the priest Isaac with his own hand, and that the gendarmes had laid wagers in firing at his clerical headdress. "I made the best shooting, hit the hat and knocked it off his head, finishing him with a second ball." My answer was silence. The man firmly believed that these murders were necessary, the Sultan having so ordered.

The Sale of Letters.—When the Government first commenced the deportation of the 700 men, the officials were instructed to prepare letters, signed with the names of the former, and to send them to the families of the banished individuals in order to mislead them, as it was feared that the Armenians might take some action which would defeat the plan and divulge the secret to the other Armenians, thus rendering their extermination impracticable. The unhappy families gave large sums to those who brought them letters from their Head. The Government appointed a Kurd, a noted brigand, as officer of the Militia, ordering him to slaughter the Armenians and deliver the letters at their destination. When the Government was secure as to the Armenians, a man was despatched to kill the Kurd, whose name was Aami Hassi, or Hassi Aami.

Slaughter of the Protestant, Chaldean, and Syriac Communities.—The slaughter was general throughout these communities, not a single protestant remaining in Diarbekir. Eighty families of the Syriac Community were exterminated, with a part of the Chaldeans, in Diarbekir, and in its dependencies, none escaped save those in Madiât and Mardîn. When latterly orders were given that only Armenians were to be killed, and that those belonging to other communities should not be touched, the Government held their hand from the destruction of the latter.

The Syriacs.—But the Syriacs in the province of Madiât were brave men, braver than all the other tribes in these regions. When they heard what had fallen upon their brethren at Diarbekir and the vicinity they assembled, fortified themselves in three villages near Madiât, and made a heroic resistance, showing a courage beyond description. The Government sent against them two companies of regulars, besides a company of gendarmes which had been despatched thither previously; the Kurdish tribes assembled against them, but without result, and thus they protected their lives, honour, and possessions from the tyranny of this oppressive Government. An Imperial Irâdeh was issued, granting them pardon, but they placed no reliance on it and did not surrender, for past experience had shown them that this is the most false Government on the face of the earth, taking back to-day what it gave yesterday, and punishing to-day with most cruel penalties him whom it had previously pardoned.

Conversation between a postal contractor from Bitlis and a friend of mine, as we were sitting at a café in Diarbekir:

Contractor: I see many Armenians in Diarbekir. How comes it that they are still here?

25

My Friend: These are not Armenians, but Syriacs and Chaldeans.

Contractor: The Government of Bitlis has not left a single Christian in that Vilayet, nor in the district of Moush. If a doctor told a sick man that the remedy for his disease was the heart of a Christian he would not find one though he searched through the whole Vilayet.

Protection Afforded by Kurds to Armenians on Payment.— The Armenians were confined in the main ward of the prison at Diarbekir, and from time to time I visited them. One day, on waking from sleep, I went to see them in their ward and found them collecting rice, flour and moneys. I asked them the reason of this, and they said: "What are we to do? If we do not collect a quantity every week and give it to the Kurds, they insult and beat us, so we give these things to some of them so that they may protect us from the outrages of their fellows." I exclaimed, "There is no power nor might but in God," and went back grieving over their lot.

Despatch of the Armenians to the Slaughter.—This was a most shocking proceeding, appalling in its atrocity. One of the gendarmes in Diarbekir related to me how it was done. He said that, when orders were given for the removal and destruction of a family, an official went to the house, counted the members of the family, and delivered them to the Commandant of Militia or one of the officers of Gendarmerie. Men were posted to keep guard over the house and its occupants during the night until 8 o'clock, thereby giving notice to the wretched family that they must prepare for death. The women shrieked and wailed, anguish and despair showed on the faces of all, and they died even before death came upon them. ... After 8 o'clock

26

waggons arrived and conveyed the families to a place near by, where they were killed by rifle fire, or massacred like sheep with knives, daggers, and axes.

Sale of Armenian Effects, and Removal of Crosses from the Churches.—After the Armenians had been destroyed, all the furniture of their houses, their linen, effects, and implements of all kinds, as well as all the contents of their shops and storehouses, were collected in the churches or other large buildings. The authorities appointed committees for the sale of these goods, which were disposed of at the lowest price, as might be the case with the effects of those who died a natural death, but with this difference, that the money realised went to the Treasury of the Turkish Government, instead of to the heirs of the deceased.

You might see a carpet, worth thirty pounds, sold for five, a man's costume, worth four pounds, sold for two medjidies, and so on with the rest of the articles, this being especially the case with musical instruments, such as pianos, etc., which had no value at all. All money and valuables were collected by the Commandant of Gendarmerie and the Vali, Reshîd Bey, the latter taking them with him when he went to Constantinople, and delivering them to Talaat Bey.[4] ...

The mind is confounded by the reflection that this people of Armenia, this brave race who astonished the world by their courage, resolution, progress and knowledge, who yesterday were the most powerful and most highly cultivated of the Ottoman peoples, have become merely a memory, as though they had never flourished. Their

---

[4] Some remarks in this connection are omitted.—Translator.

27

learned books are waste paper, used to wrap up cheese or dates, and I was told that one high official had bought thirty volumes of French literature for 50 piastres. Their schools are closed, after being thronged with pupils. Such is the evil end of the Armenian race: let it be a warning to those peoples who are striving for freedom, and let them understand that freedom is not to be achieved but by the shedding of blood, and that words are the stock-in-trade of the weak alone.

I observed that the crosses had been removed from the lofty steeples of the churches, which are used as storehouses and markets for the keeping and sale of the effects of the dead.

Methods of Slaughter.—These were of various kinds. An officer told me that in the Vilayet of Bitlis the authorities collected the Armenians in barns full of straw (or chaff), piling up straw in front of the door and setting it on fire, so that the Armenians inside perished in the smoke. He said that sometimes hundreds were put together in one barn. Other modes of killing were also employed (at Bitlis). He told me, to my deep sorrow, how he had seen a girl hold her lover in her embrace, and so enter the barn to meet her death without a tremor.

At Moush, a part were killed in straw-barns, but the greater number by shooting or stabbing with knives, the Government hiring butchers, who received a Turkish pound each day as wages. A doctor, named Azîz Bey, told me that when he was at Marzifûn, in the Vilayet of Sivas, he heard that a caravan of Armenians was being sent to execution. He went to the Kaimakâm and said to him: "You know I am a doctor, and there is no difference between doctors and butchers, as doctors are mostly

28

occupied in cutting up mankind. And as the duties of a Kaimakâm at this time are also like our own—cutting up human bodies—I beg you to let me see this surgical operation myself." Permission was given, and the doctor went. He found four butchers, each with a long knife; the gendarmes divided the Armenians into parties of ten, and sent them up to the butchers one by one. The butcher told the Armenian to stretch out his neck; he did so, and was slaughtered like a sheep. The doctor was amazed at their steadfastness in presence of death, not saying a word, or showing any sign of fear.

The gendarmes used also to bind the women and children and throw them down from a very lofty eminence, so that they reached the ground shattered to pieces. This place is said to be between Diarbekir and Mardîn, and the bones of the slain are there in heaps to this day.

Another informant told me that the Diarbekir authorities had killed the Armenians either by shooting, by the butchers, or at times by putting numbers of them in wells and caves, which were blocked up so that they perished. Also they threw them into the Tigris and the Euphrates, and the bodies caused an epidemic of typhus fever. Two thousand Armenians were slaughtered at a place outside the walls of Diarbekir, between the Castle of Sultan Murad and the Tigris, and at not more than half an hour's distance from the city.

Brutality of the Gendarmes and Kurdish Tribes.—There is no doubt that what is related as to the proceedings of the gendarmes and the Kurdish tribes actually took place. On receiving a caravan of Armenians the gendarmes searched them one by one, men and women, taking any money they might find, and stripping them of the better portions of their clothing. When they were satisfied that there remained no money, good clothes, or other things of value, they sold the Armenians in thousands to the Kurds, on the stipulation that none should be left alive. The price was in accordance with the number of the party; I was told by a reliable informant of cases where the price had varied between 2,000 and 200 liras.

After purchasing the caravans, the Kurds stripped all the Armenians, men and women, of their clothes, so that they remained entirely naked. They then shot them down, every one, after which they cut open their stomachs to search for money amongst the entrails, also cutting up the clothing, boots, etc., with the same object.

Such were the dealings of the official gendarmerie and the Kurds with their fellow-creatures. The reason of the sale of the parties by the gendarmes was to save themselves trouble, and to obtain delivery of further parties to plunder of their money.

Woe to him who had teeth of gold, or gold-plated. The gendarmes and Kurds used to violently draw out his teeth before arriving at the place of execution, thus inflicting tortures before actual death.

A Kurdish Agha Slaughters 50,000 Armenians.—A Kurd told me that the authorities of Kharpout handed over to one of the Kurdish Aghas in that Vilayet, in three batches, more than 50,000 Armenians from Erzeroum, Trebizond, Sivas, and Constantinople, with orders to kill them and to divide with themselves the property which he might take from them. He killed them all and took from them their money and other belongings. He hired 600 mules for the women, to convey them to Urfa, at the rate of three liras a head. After receiving the price, he collected mules belonging to his tribe, mounted the women on them, and brought them to a place between Malatîya and Urfa, where he killed them in the most barbarous way, taking all their money, clothes, and valuables.

The Violation of Women before or after Death.—[5] ...

Incident of the Sheikh and the Girl.—I said above that the Armenian women were sent off in batches under guard of gendarmes. Whenever they passed by a village the inhabitants would come and choose any they desired, taking them away and giving a small sum to the gendarmes. At one place a Kurd of over 60 picked out a beautiful girl of 16. She refused to have anything to do with him, but said she was ready to embrace Islam and marry a youth of her own age. This the Kurds would not allow, but gave her the choice between death and the Sheikh; she still refused, and was killed.

Barsoum Agha.—Whilst I was Kaimakâm of the district of Kiakhta, in the Vilayet of Kharpout, I was acquainted with an Armenian Notable of that place, named Barsoum Agha. He was a worthy and courageous man, dealing well with Kurds, Turks, and Armenians, without distinction; he also showed much kindness to officials who were dismissed from their posts in the district. All the Kurdish Aghas thereabouts kept close watch over him, hating him because he was their rival in the supremacy of the place. When, after my banishment, I arrived at Sivrek and heard what had befallen the Armenians, I enquired about him and his family. I was told that when the Government disposed of the Armenians of Kiakhta he was summoned

---

[5] I refrain from particulars. The gendarmes and Kurds are stated to have been the perpetrators of these acts.—Translator.

and ordered to produce the records of moneys owing to him (Kurds and Armenians in that district owed him a sum of 10,000 liras); he replied that he had torn up the records and released his debtors from their obligations. He was taken away with the other Armenians, and on arrival at the Euphrates he asked permission to drown himself. This was granted, and he endeavoured to do so, but failed, as he could not master himself. So he said to the gendarmes, "Life is dear and I cannot kill myself, so do as you have been ordered," whereupon one of them shot him and then killed the rest of the family.

Narrative of a Young Turk.—This youth, who had come to Diarbekir as a schoolmaster, told me that the Government had informed the Armenians of Broussa that their deportation had been decided, and that they were to leave for Mosul, Syria, or El-Deir three days after receiving the order. After selling what they could, they hired carts and carriages for the transport of their goods and themselves and started—as they thought—for their destination. On their arrival at a very rugged and barren place, far distant from any villages, the drivers, in conformity with their instructions, broke up the conveyances and left the people in the waste, returning in the night to plunder them. Many died there of hunger and terror; a great part were killed on the road; and only a few reached Syria or El-Deir.

Children Perishing of Hunger and Thirst.—An Arab of El-Jezîra, who accompanied me on my flight from Diarbekir, told me that he had gone with a Sheikh of his tribe, men and camels, to buy grain from the sons of Ibrahim Pasha El-Mellili. On their way they saw 17 children, the eldest not more than 13 years old, dying of hunger and thirst. The Arab said: "We had with us a small water-skin and a little food. When the Sheikh saw them he wept with pity,

32

and gave them food and water with his own hands; but what good could this small supply do to them? We reflected that if we took them with us to the Pasha, they would be killed, as the Kurds were killing all Armenians by order of the authorities; and our Arabs were at five days' distance from the place. So we had no choice but to leave them to the mercy of God, and on our return, a week later, we found them all dead."

Narrative of a Provincial Governor.—We were talking of the courage and good qualities of the Armenians, and the Governor of the place, who was with us, told us a singular story. He said: "According to orders, I collected all the remaining Armenians, consisting of 17 women and some children, amongst whom was a child of 3 years old, diseased, who had never been able to walk. When the butchers began slaughtering the women and the turn of the child's mother came, he rose up on his feet and ran for a space, then falling down. We were astonished at this, and at his understanding that his mother was to be killed. A gendarme went and took hold of him, and laid him dead on his dead mother." He also said that he had seen one of these women eating a piece of bread as she went up to the butcher, another smoking a cigarette, and that it was as though they cared nothing for death.

Narrative of Shevket Bey.—Shevket Bey, one of the officials charged with the extermination of the Armenians, told me, in company with others, the following story: "I was proceeding with a party, and when we had arrived outside the walls of Diarbekir and were beginning to shoot down the Armenians, a Kurd came up to me, kissed my hand, and begged me to give him a girl of about ten years old. I stopped the firing and sent a gendarme to bring the girl to me. When she came I pointed out a spot to her and said, 'Sit there. I have given you to this man, and you will be saved from death.' After a while, I saw that she had thrown herself amongst the dead Armenians, so I ordered the gendarmes to cease firing and bring her up. I said to her, 'I have had pity on you and brought you out from among the others to spare your life. Why do you throw yourself with them? Go with this man and he will bring you up like a daughter.' She said: 'I am the daughter of an Armenian; my parents and kinsfolk are killed among these; I will have no others in their place, and I do not wish to live any longer without them.' Then she cried and lamented; I tried hard to persuade her, but she would not listen, so I let her go her way. She left me joyfully, put herself between her father and mother, who were at the last gasp, and she was killed there." And he added: "If such was the behaviour of the children, what was that of their elders?"

Price of Armenian Women.—A reliable informant from Deir-el-Zûr told me that one of the officials of that place had bought from the gendarmes three girls for a quarter of a medjidie dollar each. Another man told me that he had bought a very beautiful girl for one lira, and I heard that among the tribes Armenian women were sold like pieces of old furniture, at low prices, varying from one to ten liras, or from one to five sheep.[6] ...

The Mutesarrif and the Armenian Girl.—On the arrival of a batch of Armenians at Deir-el-Zûr from Ras-el-Ain, the Mutesarrif desired to choose a servant-girl from amongst the women. His eye fell on a handsome girl, and he went up to her, but on his approach she turned white and was about to fall. He told her not to be afraid, and ordered his

---

[6] An unimportant anecdote omitted.—Translator.

servant to take her to his house. On returning thither he asked the reason for her terror of him, and she told him that she and her mother had been sent from Ras-el-Ain in charge of a Circassian gendarme, many other Armenian women being with them. On the way, the gendarme called her mother, and told her to give him her money, or he would kill her; she said she had none, so he tortured her till she gave him six liras.[7] ... He said to her: "You liar! You [Armenians] never cease lying. You have seen what has befallen, and will befall, all Armenians, but you will not take warning, so I shall make you an example to all who see you." Then he cut off her hands with his dagger, one after the other, then both her feet, all in sight of her daughter, whom he then took aside and violated, whilst her mother, in a dying state, witnessed the act. "And when I saw you approach me, I remembered my mother's fate and dreaded you, thinking that you would treat me as the gendarme treated my mother and myself, before each other's eyes." [8] ...

"The Reward of Hard Labour."—The Turks had collected all those of military age and dispersed amongst the battalions to perform their army service. When the Government determined on the deportation and destruction of the Armenians—as stated in their official declaration—orders were given for the formation of separate battalions of Armenians, to be employed on roads and municipal works. The battalions were formed and sent to the roads and other kinds of hard labour. They were employed in this manner for eight months, when the severity of winter set in. The Government, being then unable to make further use of them, despatched them to Diarbekir. Before their arrival, the officers telegraphed

---

[7] Unfit for reproduction.—Translator.
[8] Unimportant anecdote omitted.—Translator.

that the Armenian troops were on their way, and the authorities sent gendarmes, well furnished with cartridges, to meet the poor wretches. The gendarmes received them with rifle-fire, and 840 men perished in this manner, shot close to the city of Diarbekir.

A Caravan of Women.— [9] ...

A Night's Shelter for Fifty Pounds.—The man who showed the greatest capacity for exterminating Armenians was Reshîd Bey, the Vali of Diarbekir. I have already stated how many were killed in his Vilayet. When news of his removal arrived, the remaining Armenians, and the Christians generally rejoiced, and shortly after the report was current some Armenians, who had hidden themselves, came out from their concealment and walked about the city. The Vali, who was anxious to keep his removal secret and to inspire terror, began deporting Armenians with still greater energy, and those who had come out returned to their hiding-places. One of the principal men of Diarbekir stated that one Armenian had paid fifty Turkish pounds to an inhabitant for shelter in his house during the night before the Vali's departure, and another told me that a man had received an offer of three pounds for each night until the same event, but had refused from fear of the authorities.

Chastity of the Armenian Women.— [10] ... An Arab of the Akidât told me that he was going along the bank of the

---

[9] Unimportant. The writer describes the inhabitants of Diarbekir, on the arrival of a party, as hastening to select women. Two doctors pick out twenty of them to serve as hospital attendants.—Translator.

[10] An official relates how he wanted to choose a servant from a boatload of victims, who said they were willing to come as servants, but as nothing else. He took one, and on coming home one night drunk he tried to offer her

Euphrates when he saw some of the town rabble stripping two women of their clothes. He expostulated and told them to restore the clothes, but they paid no attention. The women begged for mercy, and finding it unavailing they threw themselves into the river, preferring death to dishonour. He told me also of another woman who had a suckling child, and begged food from the passers-by, who were in too great fear of the authorities to help her. On the third day of starvation, finding no relief, she left the baby in the market of El-Deir and drowned herself in the Euphrates. In this way do they show high qualities, honour, and courage such as many men do not possess.

Women-Servants in Diarbekir.—You cannot enter a house in Diarbekir without finding from one to five Armenian maid-servants, even the humblest shopkeepers having one, who probably in the lifetime of her parents would not have condescended to speak a word to the master whom she now has to serve in order to save her life. It is stated that the number of such women and girls in the city is over 5,000, mostly from Erzeroum, Kharpout and other Vilayets.

Narrative of Shahîn Bey.—Shahîn Bey, a man of Diarbekir, who was in prison with me, told me that a number of Armenian men and women were delivered to him for slaughter, he being a soldier. He said: "Whilst we were on the way, I saw an Armenian girl whom I knew, and who was very beautiful. I called her by name, and said 'Come, I will save you, and you shall marry a young man of your country, a Turk or a Kurd.' She refused, and said: 'If you wish to do me a kindness I will ask one thing which you may do for me.' I told her I would do whatever she wished,

---

violence; she reproved him in suitable terms and he conducted himself well thenceforward.—Translator.

and she said: 'I have a brother, younger than myself, here amongst these people. I pray you to kill him before you kill me, so that in dying I may not be anxious in mind about him.' She pointed him out and I called him. When he came, she said to him, 'My brother, farewell. I kiss you for the last time, but we shall meet, if it be God's will, in the next world, and He will soon avenge us for what we have suffered.' They kissed each other, and the boy delivered himself to me. I must needs obey my orders, so I struck him one blow with an axe, split his skull, and he fell dead. Then she said: 'I thank you with all my heart, and shall ask you one more favour'; she put her hands over her eyes and said: 'Strike as you struck my brother, one blow, and do not torture me.' So I struck one blow and killed her, and to this day I grieve over her beauty and youth, and her wonderful courage."

Photographs of Armenians lying in the road, dressed in turbans, for despatch to Constantinople. The Turkish Government thought that European nations might get to hear of the destruction of the Armenians and publish the news abroad so as to excite prejudice against the Turks. So after the gendarmes had killed a number of Armenian men, they put on them turbans and brought Kurdish women to weep and lament over them, saying that the Armenians had killed their men. They also brought a photographer to photograph the bodies and the weeping women, so that at a future time they might be able to convince Europe that it was the Armenians who had attacked the Kurds and killed them, that the Kurdish tribes had risen against them in revenge, and that the Turkish Government had had no part in the matter. But the secret of these proceedings was not hidden from men of intelligence, and after all this had been done, the truth became known and was spread abroad in Diarbekir.

Conversion of Armenian Women to Islam.—When the Government undertook the extermination of the Armenians some of the women went to the Mufti and the Kadi, and declared their desire to embrace the Mohammedan faith. These authorities accepted their conversion, and they were married to men of Diarbekir, either Turks or Kurds.

After a while, the Government began to collect these women, so the Mufti and the Kadi went to the Vali and said that the women in question were no longer Armenians, having become Mussulmans, and that by the Sacred Law the killing of Mussulman women was not permissible. The Vali replied: "These women are vipers, who will bite us in time to come; do not oppose the Government in this matter, for politics have no religion, and the Government know what they are about." The Mufti and the Kadi went back as they had come, and the women were sent to death. After the removal of the Vali— in consequence, as it was said, of abuses in connection with the sale of effects left in Armenian houses and shops—orders arrived that the conversion of any who desired to enter Islam should be accepted, be they men or women. Many of the Armenians who remained, of both sexes, hastened to embrace the Faith in the hope of saving their lives, but after a time they were despatched likewise and their Islamism did not save them.

The Germans and the Armenians.—Whenever the talk fell on the Armenians I used to blame the Turks for their proceedings, but one day when we were discussing the question, an official of Diarbekir, who was one of the fanatical Young Turk Nationalists, said: "The Turks are not to blame in this matter, for the Germans were the first to apply this treatment to the Poles, who were under their rule. And the Germans have compelled the Turks to take this course, saying that if they did not kill the Armenians there would be no alliance with them, and thus Turkey had no choice."

This is what the Turk said, word for word. And it was confirmed by what I heard from a Turk who was imprisoned with me at Aalîya, on the charge of corresponding with Abdul-Kerîm el-Khalîl. He said that when passing through Damascus he had visited the German Vice-Consul there, who had told him confidentially that Oppenheim had come on a special mission, which was to incite Jemâl Pasha to persecute the Arabs, with a view to causing hatred between the two races, by which the Germans might profit in future if differences arose between them and the Turks. This was a short time previous to the execution of Abdul-Kerîm.

The Killing of the Two Kaimakâms.—When the Government at Diarbekir gave orders to the officials to kill the Armenians, a native of Baghdad was Kaimakâm of El-Beshîri, in that Vilayet, and an Albanian was Kaimakâm of Lîjeh. These two telegraphed to the Vilayet that their consciences would not permit them to do such work, and that they resigned their posts. Their resignations were accepted, but they were both secretly assassinated. I investigated this matter carefully, and ascertained that the name of the Baghdad Arab was Sabat Bey El-Sueidi, but I could not learn that of the Albanian, which I much regret, as they performed a noble act for which they should be commemorated in history.... [11]

---

[11] The writer here describes how a Turkish judge (kâdi), to whom the office of Kaimakâm was entrusted after the murder of Sabat Bey, boasted in conversation that he had killed four Armenians with his own hand. "They were brave men," he said, "having no fear of death."—Translator.

An Armenian Betrays His Nation.— [12] ...

The Sultan's Order.—Whilst I was in prison, a Turkish Commissioner of Police used to come to see a friend of his, who was also imprisoned. One day when I and this friend were together, the Commissioner came, and, in the course of conversation about the Armenians and their fate, he described to us how he had slaughtered them, and how a number had taken refuge in a cave outside the city, and he had brought them out and killed two of them himself. His friend said to him: "Have you no fear of God? Whence have you the right to take life in defiance of God's law?" He replied: "It was the Sultan's order; the Sultan's order is the order of God, and its fulfilment is a duty."

Armenian Death Statistics.—At the end of August, 1915, I was visited in prison by one of my Diarbekir colleagues, who was an intimate friend of one of those charged with the conduct of the Armenian massacres. We spoke of the Armenian question, and he told me that, in Diarbekir alone, 570,000 had been destroyed, these being people from other Vilayets as well as those belonging to Diarbekir itself.

If to this we add those killed in the following months, amounting to about 50,000; and those in the Vilayets of Bitlis and Van and the province of Moush, approximately 230,000; and those who perished in Erzeroum, Kharpout, Sivas, Stamboul, Trebizond, Adana, Broussa, Urfa, Zeitoun, and Aintab—estimated at upwards of 350,000—

---

[12] The author tells the story of an Armenian of Diarbekir who gave information to the police against his own people, disclosing their hiding places. He saw him walking about the streets with an insolent demeanor, giving himself the airs of a person of great importance. He considers that such a traitor to his nation deserves the worst form of death.—Translator.

we arrive at a total of Armenians killed, or dead from disease, hunger, or thirst, of 1,200,000.

There remain 300,000 Armenians in the Vilayet of Aleppo, in Syria, and Deir-el-Zûr (those deported thither), and in America and Egypt and elsewhere; and 400,000 in Roumelian territory, held by the Balkan States, thus making a grand total of 1,900,000.

The above is what I was able to learn as to the statistics of the slaughtered Armenians, and I would quote an extract from El-Mokattam, dealing with this subject:

"The Basle correspondent of the Temps states that, according to official reports received from Aleppo in the beginning of 1916, there were 492,000 deported Armenians in the districts of Mosul, Diarbekir, Aleppo, Damascus, and Deir-el-Zûr. The Turkish Minister of the Interior, Talaat Bey, estimates the number of deportees at 800,000, and states that 300,000 of these have been removed or have died in the last few months.

"Another calculation gives the number of deported Armenians as 1,200,000 souls, and states that at least 500,000 have been killed or have died in banishment" (El-Mokattam, May 30th, 1916).

The Armenians and the Arab Tribes.—As I approached Diarbekir, I passed through many Arab tribes, with whom I saw a number of Armenians, men and women, who were being well treated, although the Government had let the tribes know that the killing of Armenians was a bounden duty. I did not hear of a single instance of an Armenian being murdered or outraged by a tribesman, but I heard that some Arabs, passing by a well into which men and women had been thrown, drew them out when at the last extremity, took them with them, and tended them till they were recovered.

The Arab and the Armenian Beggar Woman.— [13] ...

---

[13] The narrative concludes with the relation of an instance of courageous charity on the part of a Baghdad soldier to an Armenian woman begging in the streets of Diarbekir.—Translator

# CONCLUSION

If the Turkish Government were asked the reasons for
which the Armenian men, women, and children were
killed, and their honour and property placed at any man's
mercy, they would reply that this people have murdered
Moslems in the Vilayet of Van, and that there have been
found in their possession prohibited arms, explosive
bombs, and indications of steps towards the formation of
an Armenian State, such as flags and the like, all pointing
to the fact that this race has not turned from its evil ways,
but on the first opportunity will kill the Moslems, rise in
revolt, and invoke the help of Russia, the enemy of
Turkey, against its rulers. That is what the Turkish
Government would say. I have followed the matter from its
source. I have enquired from inhabitants and officials of
Van, who were in Diarbekir, whether any Moslem had
been killed by Armenians in the town of Van, or in the
districts of the Vilayet. They answered in the negative,
saying that the Government had ordered the population to
quit the town before the arrival of the Russians and before
anyone was killed; but that the Armenians had been
summoned to give up their arms and had not done so,
dreading an attack by the Kurds, and dreading the
Government also; the Government had further demanded
that the principal Notables and leading men should be
given up to them as hostages, but the Armenians had not
complied.

All this took place during the approach of the Russians
towards the city of Van. As to the adjacent districts, the
authorities collected the Armenians and drove them into

44

the interior, where they were all slaughtered, no Government official or private man, Turk or Kurd, having been killed.

As regards Diarbekir, you have read the whole story in this book, and no insignificant event took place there, let alone murders or breaches of the peace, which could lead the Turkish Government to deal with the Armenians in this atrocious manner.

At Constantinople, we hear of no murder or other unlawful act committed by the Armenians, except the unauthenticated story about the twenty bravoes, to which I have already referred.

They have not done the least wrong in the Vilayets of Kharpout, Trebizond, Sivas, Adana, or Bitlis, nor in the province of Moush.

I have related the episode at Zeitoun, which was unimportant, and that at Urfa, where they acted in self-defence, seeing what had befallen their people, and preferring death to surrender.

As to their preparations, the flags, bombs and the like, even assuming there to be some truth in the statement, it does not justify the annihilation of the whole people, men and women, old men and children, in a way which revolts all humanity and more especially Islam and the whole body of Moslems, as those unacquainted with the true facts might impute these deeds to Mohammedan fanaticism.

To such as assert this it will suffice to point out the murders and oppressive acts committed by the Young

Turks against Islam in Syria and Mesopotamia. In Syria they have hanged the leading men of enlightenment, without fault on their part, such as Shukri Bey El-Asli, Abdul-Wahhâb Bey El-Inglîzi, Selîm Bey El-Jezairi, Emir Omar El-Husseini, Abdul-Ghani El-Arîsi, Shefîk Bey El-Moweyyad, Rushdi Bey El-Shamaa, Abdul-Hamîd El-Zahrâwi, Abdul-Kerîm El-Khalîl, Emir Aarif El-Shehâbi, Sheikh Ahmed Hasan Tabâra, and more than thirty leading men of this class.

I have published this pamphlet in order to refute beforehand inventions and slanders against the faith of Islam and against Moslems generally, and I affirm that what the Armenians have suffered is to be attributed to the Committee of Union and Progress, who deal with the empire as they please; it has been due to their nationalist fanaticism and their jealousy of the Armenians, and to these alone; the Faith of Islam is guiltless of their deeds.

From the foregoing we know that the Armenians have committed no acts justifying the Turks in inflicting on them this horrible retribution, unprecedented even in the dark ages. What, then, was the reason which impelled the Turkish Government to kill off a whole people, of whom they used to say that they were their brothers in patriotism, the principal factor in bringing about the downfall of the despotic rule of Abdul-Hamîd and the introduction of the Constitution, loyal to the Empire, and fighting side by side with the Turks in the Balkan war? The Turks sanctioned and approved the institution of Armenian political societies, which they did not do in the case of other nationalities.

What is the reason of this sudden change of attitude?

It is that, previous to the proclamation of the Constitution, the Unionists hated despotic rule; they preached equality, and inspired the people with hatred of the despotism of Abdul-Hamîd. But as soon as they had themselves seized the reins of authority, and tasted the sweets of power, they found that despotism was the best means to confirm themselves in ease and prosperity, and to limit to the Turks alone the rule over the Ottoman peoples. On considering these peoples, they found that the Armenian race was the only one which would resent their despotism, and fight against it as they previously fought against Abdul-Hamîd. They perceived also that the Armenians excelled all the other races in arts and industries, that they were more advanced in learning and societies, and that after a while the greater part of the officers of the army would be Armenians. They were confounded at this, and dreaded what might ensue, for they knew their own weakness and that they could not rival the Armenians in the way of learning and progress. Annihilation seemed to them to be the sole means of deliverance; they found their opportunity in a time of war, and they proceeded to this atrocious deed, which they carried out with every circumstance of brutality—a deed which is contrary to the law of Islam, as is shown by many precepts and historical instances. [14] ...

In view of this, how can the Turkish Government be justified at the present time in killing off an entire people, who have always paid their dues of every kind to the Ottoman State, and have never rebelled against it? Even if we suppose the Armenian men to have been deserving of death, what was the offence of the women and children?

---

[14] Fà'iz El-Ghusein here gives a list of citations from the Koran, the Traditions, and from Moslem history in support of this view.—Translator.

And what will be the punishment of those who killed them wrongfully and consumed the innocent with fire?

I am of opinion that the Mohammedan peoples are now under the necessity of defending themselves, for unless Europeans are made acquainted with the true facts they will regard this deed as a black stain on the history of Islam, which ages will not efface.

From the Verses, Traditions, and historical instances, it is abundantly clear that the action of the Turkish Government has been in complete contradiction to the principles of the Faith of Islam; a Government which professes to be the protector of Islam, and claims to hold the Khilâfat, cannot act in opposition to Moslem law; and a Government which does so act is not an Islamic Government, and has no rightful pretension to be such.

It is incumbent on the Moslems to declare themselves guiltless of such a Government, and not to render obedience to those who trample under foot the Verses of the Koran and the Traditions of the Prophet, and shed the innocent blood of women, old men and infants, who have done no wrong. Otherwise they make themselves accomplices in this crime, which stands unequalled in history.

In conclusion, I would address myself to the Powers of Europe, and say that it is they themselves who have encouraged the Turkish Government to this deed, for they were aware of the evil administration of that Government, and its barbarous proceedings on many occasions in the past, but did not check it.

Completed at Bombay on the 3rd September, 1916.
FÀ'IZ EL-GHUSEIN.